A Love Affair With Hummus: Classic and Delicious Hummus Recipes

by Rachel Lane

Contents

What's the Big Deal About Hummus?

If I had to pick a favorite food (and thank God I don't), hummus would be pretty close to the top of the list. I could probably eat hummus every day of my life without tiring of it. It's that good.

It goes good with sandwiches, works great as a healthy dip and is an awesome spread. You'd be hard-pressed to find something that can't be made better with hummus.

There are a ton of recipes and variations of hummus out floating around out there. I've made it my personal mission to try each and every single one of them. I'm not quite there, but I've got to be getting close.

The Chickpea (or Whatever You Want to Call It)

In Spain, they're called garbanzo beans. In Italy, cece beans. Call them what you want, chickpeas are essential to pretty much every hummus recipe. There's only one recipe in this entire book that doesn't use chickpeas.

The chickpea is a powerhouse when it comes to nutrition and diet. What was once a Middle Eastern secret is now being recognized world-wide as one of the healthiest foods around.

It's not only healthy, it's delicious when made into hummus. Kids and adults alike love it and it's cheap and easy to make. It takes about 10 minutes to whip up a batch of hummus that will last you days.

Dry or Canned?

Chickpeas can be bought in cans or as dry beans that need to be soaked overnight and cooked the next day. The dry beans are slightly better for you, but the canned ones are much easier to prepare. It's estimated that you can lose up to 20% of the nutrients when you go with canned beans over the dry beans that have to be soaked. It's up to you to decide if this is a fair trade-off.

If the convenience of using canned beans means you're more likely to make and eat hummus, then go with the canned beans. You aren't going to get any nutritional value from hummus you don't make and eat.

Skinned or Unskinned?

The next decision you need to make is whether or not you're going to skin the beans. Skinned beans make for smoother hummus and are easier to digest. If you decide to skin the beans, drain them after cooking them until they start to get a little soft and place them in cold water. Many of the skins will slide right off. To get the tougher ones off, pinch the bean between two fingers. The bean should pop out of the skin when you apply a little pressure. Bring the beans back to a boil and cook until soft.

Health Benefits of Hummus

Hummus is healthy.

It's full of fiber, and the fiber in hummus is more beneficial to the human body than the fiber derived from most other sources. The fiber found in chickpeas is insoluble fiber.

What this means is the fiber won't begin to break down when it comes in contact with the fluids and acids found in your stomach. It makes its way down to your large intestines before it starts to break down. Since this is a recipe book and not a medical science book, I'm not going to get into the finer details-- let's just say the longer fiber takes to break down, the better it is for you.

The fiber found in chickpeas is good for you. There's also a lot of it. A single cup of chickpeas contains almost 13 grams of insoluble fiber. This is roughly equal to half of the fiber intake the human body needs daily.

Fiber isn't the only good thing in hummus. The chickpeas found in hummus are also high in antioxidants. One cup of hummus provides you with more than 3/4 of your daily recommended intake of manganese, one of the stronger antioxidants your body needs.

The good stuff doesn't stop here. Hummus has been shown to lower cholesterol and help regulate blood sugar. It also contains chemicals called isoflavones, which are plant chemicals that can help treat hormone-related stress.

Preparing Dried Garbanzos

Dried garbanzo beans are widely believed to be one of the tougher beans to cook. The reason for this is they don't always soften up the way they need to in order to make good hummus. The truth is that this isn't because the beans are hard to cook; it's because the beans used have been left sitting for too long.

Dried up, shriveled beans are going to be next to impossible to soften up. Make sure you get your beans from a store that sells a lot of them and doesn't have a bunch of old stock sitting on the shelves.

Once you find a good bag of beans, it's time to soak them. Cover them with water and let sit overnight. It takes around 10 hours for chickpeas to soak enough to where they're ready to cook.

Once the beans have soaked overnight, place them in pot of water and boil them until soft. Alternatively, you can put them in a slow cooker and bring them to a slow boil. Cook as long as it takes for them to soften. I'm intentionally not giving you a set time because it may take quite some time for older beans to soften, while fresh beans will soften quickly. Check them once every half hour or so to see if they're ready.

If you decide to peel them, do it right after they begin to soften up a bit. If you wait too long, it's going to be tough to get the stuck skins off of the tougher beans.

Tahini is Good Stuff Too

Most hummus recipes also call for Tahini. While it's often used in hummus, most people have no clue what it is or how it's made.

Tahini is a paste that's made from sesame seeds. You can buy it already made or, if you're feeling industrious, you can make it yourself. Here's a quick recipe for the Tahini paste used in hummus:

Add 1/2 cup raw Tahini and a little bit of water to a small bowl. Slowly add water and stir until it becomes the texture of a thick paste. Add the juice from half a lemon, 1 minced clove of garlic and a stalk of celery that's been finely chopped. Add a pinch or two of salt, to taste and stir. If the mixture is too thick, gradually add water while stirring.

Tahini adds even more nutritional value to your hummus. A quarter cup of sesame seeds contains up to 70 percent of your daily recommended value of copper and more than a quarter of your recommended intake of calcium and magnesium.

Tahini can be eaten on its own, but it's much better mixed in hummus.

Recipes

While it's debatable whether there even is a basic hummus recipe, this is the one I use most often. I find myself using variations of this recipe frequently and I'm sure you will too. On its own, this recipe is rather bland. Don't serve it like this. Instead, use this recipe as a jumping off point for your own delicious hummus recipes!

Ingredients:

1 can chickpeas, drained and rinsed

1/4 cup liquid from chickpeas

1/4 cup Tahini

1 tbs lemon juice

2 1/2 tbs olive oil

1/2 tsp salt

1/2 tsp cumin, ground

Paprika, to taste

Directions:

Combine all of the ingredients except for the paprika in a food processor or blender and blend until a creamy consistency. Place in serving bowl and garnish with paprika to taste. The paprika can be eliminated if you don't like it.

Basic Hummus Without Tahini

Some people dislike hummus because the Tahini has too strong of a flavor. This recipe is for those people. It substitutes sesame oil for the Tahini for a milder flavor.

Ingredients:

1 can chickpeas, rinsed and dried

2 tbs olive oil

2 tbs lemon juice

1 1/2 cloves garlic, minced

1/2 tsp salt

1/2 tsp cumin

3 tbs sesame oil

1/2 tsp black pepper

3 tbs warm water

Directions:

1. Blend chickpeas, olive oil, lemon juice and garlic in a food processor.

2. Add the rest of the ingredients, then blend until a smooth consistency. The hummus should be thick, but not too dry. Add water if necessary.

Lemon Garlic Hummus

Add a little (more) kick to your hummus by adding lemon and garlic. This simple recipe is one of my favorites.

Ingredients:

1 can chickpeas, drained and rinsed

1/4 cup liquid from chickpeas

2 cloves garlic, crushed

2 1/2 tbs lemon juice

2 1/2 tbs olive oil

2 tsp Tahini

Directions:

Combine ingredients in blender or food processor and blend until smooth. This usually takes about 4 minutes on low. For added flavor when serving, create a shallow well in the hummus and add a couple teaspoons of olive oil.

Roasted-Garlic Hummus (Tahini-Free)

This recipe is Tahini-free. It's also delicious, at least for those who love garlic.

Ingredients:

1 can chickpeas, drained and rinsed

1 tbs lemon juice

2 tbs olive oil

2 tbs roasted garlic

1/2 tsp salt

1/2 tbs oregano

Parsley

Directions:

You should be pretty well-versed in how to do this by now. Blend until a smooth, paste-like consistency. Add olive oil if too dry. Sprinkle parsley on top for added flavor. If you like garlic, add more of it, to taste.

Spanish Cilantro Hummus

Not everyone likes cilantro. I do, my husband and children don't. If you're firmly in the cilantro-lovers group, this is the hummus recipe for you.

Ingredients:

1 can chickpeas, drained and rinsed

1/4 cup liquid from chickpeas

2 tbs Tahini

1 tsp cilantro, chopped

2 cloves garlic, crushed

3 tbs lemon juice

2 1/2 tbs olive oil

1/2 tsp salt

Directions:

Combine all ingredients except for the water from the chickpea can and blend. Add the water and blend until smooth.

Chipotle Cilantro Hummus

Hummus with a little kick. The chipotle adds a nice smoky flavor to the hummus. I'm going to cheat here a little with this recipe, as the ingredients and instructions are exactly the same as the previous recipe.

The only difference is that you need to add 1 teaspoon chipotle chiles, diced into tiny pieces.

Roasted Red Pepper Hummus

Has even more kick than the chipotle hummus recipe. If you like your food a tad spicy, try this hummus on for size. For best results, get fresh roasted red peppers from your local supermarket. In a pinch, canned roasted red peppers will allso work.

Ingredients:

1 can chickpeas, drained and rinsed

1/2 cup Tahini

3 tbs lemon juice

2 tbs olive oil

2 cloves garlic, crushed

1/2 tsp salt

3/4 cup roasted red peppers

Parsley

Directions:

Add all ingredients except parsley to blender or food processor and blend until smooth.

Jalapeno Hummus

This hummus is spicy. You can either leave the seeds in or remove the seeds, depending on how hot you want it to be. If you like it hot, leave the seeds in.

Ingredients:

1 can chickpeas, drained and rinsed

1 chopped jalapeno pepper

2 tbs Tahini

2 tbs lemon juice

2 tbs olive oil

2 cloves garlic, crushed

Directions:

Add the ingredients to a blender or food processor and blend until smooth.

Pumpkin Hummus

This hummus is perfect for Thanksgiving or for fall dinners. Use canned or fresh pumpkin to give the hummus its pumpkin flavor.

Ingredients:

1/2 can chickpeas, drained and rinsed

1/2 can canned pumpkin

2 tbs Tahini

2 tbs lemon juice

2 tbs olive oil

2 tbs chopped basil

1 clove garlic, crushed

1/2 tsp salt

Cinnamon

Directions:

Blend or process ingredients until smooth and creamy. Add water if too thick. Place hummus into serving bowl and sprinkle cinnamon on top for added flavor.

Zucchini Hummus

Vegetables make for a great addition to hummus. Zucchini is one of my favorite veggies to add.

Ingredients:

1 can chickpeas, drained and rinsed

1/4 cup liquid from chickpeas

2 tbs Tahini

3 tbs lemon juice

2 tbs olive oil

2 cloves garlic, crushed

1/2 tsp salt

1/2 cup zuchinni, chopped

Directions:

Combine all ingredients except for the water from the chickpea can and blend. Add the water and blend until smooth. Place in serving bowl and create a shallow well in the hummus. Add a couple teaspoons of olive oil to the hummus.

Cucumber Hummus

Cucumber adds a light, summery flavor to hummus. With this recipe, the cucumber isn't blended into the hummus. It's sliced and placed on top.

Ingredients:

1 can chickpeas, drained and rinsed

1/4 cup liquid from chickpeas

1 1/2 tbs Tahini

3 tbs lemon juice

2 tbs olive oil

2 cloves garlic, crushed

1/2 tsp salt

1 whole fresh cucumber

Directions:

Combine ingredients and blend in food processor or blender until creamy. Add liquid until consistency is like a smooth paste.

Wash the cucumber and slice into thin rounds. Place cucumber on top of hummus.

There isn't much that can't be made better with avocado, hummus included.

Ingredients:

1 can chickpeas, drained and rinsed

1/4 cup liquid from chickpeas

1 large avocado, pitted and peeled

1/4 fresh tomato, diced

2 tbs Tahini

3 tbs lemon juice

2 tbs olive oil

2 cloves garlic, crushed

1/2 tsp salt

Directions:

Spinach and Feta Hummus

This is a fairly common (and fairly delicious) variation of traditional hummus served in the Middle East. It is perfect as a spread or when used as a dip.

Ingredients:

1 can chickpeas, drained and rinsed

Feta cheese, to taste

1/4 cup red pepper flakes

1/2 cup spinach

2 tbs Tahini

3 tbs lemon juice

2 tbs olive oil

2 cloves garlic, crushed

1/2 tsp salt

Directions:

Combine the chickpeas, Tahini, garlic, spinach, olive oil and lemon juice in a blender or food processor and blend. Add the red pepper flakes and cheese and blend until smooth.

Mediterranean Hummus

The addition of tomatoes and basil give this hummus recipe a distinct Mediterranean flavor.

Ingredients:

1 can chickpeas, drained and rinsed

1/4 cup liquid from chickpeas

1 can peeled tomatoes

1/4 fresh tomato, diced

2 tbs Tahini

2 tbs lemon juice

2 tbs olive oil

1/4 tsp cumin

2 tbs chopped basil

2 cloves garlic, crushed

1/2 tsp salt

Directions:

Blend all ingredients until they are a smooth, pasty consistency.
Add diced fresh tomato to top of hummus before serving.

This is the only hummus recipe I've ever seen that doesn't use chickpeas. The only reason I decided to include it in this book is because black beans are almost as healthy as chickpeas. If you don't like chickpeas, try this recipe. Otherwise, use one of the recipes with chickpeas.

Ingredients:

1 can black beans, drained and rinsed

1/4 fresh tomato, diced

2 tbs Tahini

1 tbs lemon juice

1 tbs lime juice

2 tbs olive oil

1/4 tsp cumin

2 cloves garlic, crushed

1/2 tsp salt

Directions:

You know the routing. Blend or process all ingredients until the mixture is a creamy paste. If too thick, add a little olive oil or a little water to thin it out.

This recipe replaces the fattening Tahini with peanut butter and yogurt. I was pretty skeptical until I tried it. It's actually pretty good.

Ingredients:

1 can chickpeas, drained and rinsed

1/4 cup liquid from chickpeas

1 tbs lemon juice

2 cloves garlic, crushed

1/2 tsp salt

1/2 tsp cumin

1 tbs low-fat peanut butter

1/2 cup plain yogurt

Directions:

Combine ingredients and blend or process until a smooth paste. If too thick, add a little olive oil to thin it out.

The Best Ways to Serve Hummus

There's no doubt hummus makes a great meal. There are a number of ways to serve hummus and I'm constantly searching for new stuff that goes good with hummus.

My favorite way to eat it is in the traditional manner, served with bread or falafels. This is the way hummus has been served for thousands of years. There's no doubt it's delicious and will likely be served for another couple thousand years.

Hummus makes a good dip for raw vegetables. The following veggies go well with hummus:

- Cucumber
- Cauliflower
- Carrots
- Sugar Snap Peas
- Broccoli
- Fresh tomatoes
- Cooked asparagus
- Olives
- Fresh onions
- Cherry tomatoes
- Lettuce leaves

I recently tried replacing the filling in deviled eggs with hummus and it turned out great. The guests at my party loved it and complimented my innovative choice of filling.

Hummus also works great as a dip for tortilla or corn chips and as a sandwich spread. It can be added to a number of foods to add flavor and make them taste better. The uses of hummus are limited only by your imagination.

How to Properly Store Hummus

Hummus will keep for up to a week if stored in an airtight plastic container in the fridge. If you add a little olive oil to the top, the hummus will remain moist for a longer period of time.

Hummus can be frozen, but will lose some of its consistency and flavor if stored for a long period of time. Once you thaw it out, add a little olive oil to it, then reblend it to a smooth consistency.

A better option is to boil and peel the beans, then freeze them. When you want some hummus, add the rest of the ingredients and mix up a fresh batch. It will taste better this way and you can store the frozen beans indefinitely.

28188324R00023

Made in the USA
Lexington, KY
08 December 2013